∞

What Is Heaven?

Mother Angelica

What Is
Heaven?

EWTN PUBLISHING, INC.
Irondale, Alabama

EWTN Publishing, Inc.
5817 Old Leeds Road, Irondale, AL 35210

Distributed by Sophia Institute Press, Box 5284, Manchester, NH 03108.

Library of Congress Cataloging-in-Publication Data

Names: M. Angelica (Mary Angelica), Mother, 1923-2016, author.
Title: What is heaven / Mother Angelica.
Description: Irondale, Alabama : EWTN Publishing, Inc., 2019.
Identifiers: LCCN 2019014939 | ISBN 9781682780893 (pbk. : alk. paper)
Subjects: LCSH: Heaven—Christianity. | Catholic Church—Doctrines. |
    Theology, Doctrinal—Popular works.
Classification: LCC BT846.3 .M2 2019 | DDC 236/.24—dc23 LC record
available at https://lccn.loc.gov /2019014939

Contents

∞

Introduction

∞

Mother Angelica Live! hit the airwaves in 1983, two years after EWTN began broadcasting. The show was a gamble in several respects. First, it was an experiment in the high-wire act of live television. Second, it was a live program with a single host, on whom each show would depend. And third, that host was a cloistered nun wearing a traditional habit.

But *Mother Angelica Live!* had the most important point in its favor: The host on whom everything would depend was the funny, salty, winsome, wise, and, most importantly, prayerful Mother Mary Angelica. She understood in a profound way that, while she might seem to be in charge, each program depended first and foremost on the grace of God: Any good things that would come from her words would be His doing. And so she preceded every taping with prayer, often before the Blessed Sacrament, and entrusted everything to Him.

What Is Heaven?

Mother Angelica always had a fascination with Heaven, and so it's no surprise that she dedicated several episodes to the topic early in the show's eighteen-year run. These chapters come from seven episodes that aired in 1986, during which she taught her growing audience about the eternal beatitude God has waiting for us—should we choose it. Mother lived with that heavenly awareness that keeps everything in this life in perspective, and it comes through in the way she presents this fascinating, even mystical material.

The original episodes were delivered in Mother Angelica's distinctive, witty, extemporaneous style; the transcripts have been edited for reading clarity, but her wisdom is pure and her personality remains unquestionably her own. This is the genuine article: Mother Angelica talking to her television family—and now to you—about the highest hopes and gravest fears of humanity, a timeless voice of charity, honesty, and comfort.

∞

What Is Heaven?

Chapter 1

∞

What Is Heaven?

∞

To most of us, Heaven is rather abstract. It's a kind of fuzzy thing. Often in life, we look forward to events—graduations, doctorates, marriage, and so on. But when our anticipation is great, the event, when it occurs, seems to lose something. That's why, I believe, we don't like to talk about Heaven. We're so afraid it won't be anything like what we are expecting, and so we begin to doubt.

St. Paul said, "The things that no eye has seen and no ear has heard, things beyond the mind of man, ... God has prepared for those who love him" (1 Cor. 2:9). What Heaven is like hasn't even entered into our wildest imaginations. On earth, you and I want happiness. But life is fraught with a little bit of bitterness, even when we're happy. That's because, as soon as we have something that makes us happy, we're afraid we're going to lose it. Happiness, here on earth, is always bittersweet.

What Is Heaven?

We get so attached to this happiness that we become devastated when we lose it. That's because happiness is an oasis in the desert. When we're in that oasis, we don't want to go anywhere else. And when we leave, we don't want to think about the desert all around, so we pretend it's not there. And then, if somebody talks to us about Heaven, far off in the invisible distance, we don't want to hear it. We live in an age when we delude ourselves about where real happiness is found.

And so, although we might have glimpses of that eternal life, we're not ready for it. We don't know what it means. We want to get there immediately or in a hurry, but we can't, and so we pretend that what we have here and now is all there is. But if what we have now is all there is, we wouldn't be any different from a dog, because what he has now is really all he has. He's not going to get one thing more when he dies. I'm sorry to say that you're not going to find your dog in Heaven wagging his little tail. He doesn't have an immortal soul.

For most of us, then, keeping Heaven in our mind is difficult—especially for those of us, like me, who don't have very creative minds. We prefer the things we can see. We think, "Don't tell me what is going to be. Give it to me now!"

But let's take a look now at the question "Why do we fear death?" First, most of us are afraid of judgment. We just aren't sure if we're really sorry for our sins—or even if we remember them. That's because we haven't fully grasped the beautiful truth of God's fatherly love and comfort and forgiveness. And when God forgives, He forgives and He forgets.

And yet we are so often afraid of God and His Kingdom. Why are we afraid of a Father who is so generous and so loving and so compassionate that He's willing to give us a clean sheet? How many people give us a clean sheet? Anybody? Most people forgive, but they don't forget. There are almost always little shadows left over.

Many of the first Christians led lives of debauchery, but they had a faith that assured them that once they had a clean sheet from God after Confession, they could seek, desire, and obtain Heaven. Why? Because God is our Father. Their faith was so real that when they were put in an arena to face lions, when Peter and Andrew were crucified, when Bartholomew was flayed alive, they all relied confidently on the power of God to keep them going. When St. Stephen was stoned to death, he saw Heaven open up, and he saw Jesus at the right hand of the Father. And as they were attacking him, his face glowed like an angel and he said, "Receive my spirit.... Lord, do not hold this sin against them" (Acts 7:59–60).

We have to find out what those Christians had that we lack today, and what it is that has smothered real Christianity in our hearts. What is it in our lives that smothers the truth? What is covering it over? Is it riches? Is it a desire for human glory? Is it lust? Is it alcohol? Is it sex? Is it pride? What is it that hides the glory of the Kingdom from our eyes and makes us desire the least? What is it, or who is it, that blinds our eyes to the point where we desire to live in a mud shack rather than in a mansion? What is it in our lives that distorts the facts of life so greatly?

Holiness in this life is not complicated. It consists of one thing: the Will of God. Do you know what Our Lord told Sr. Lucy of Fatima? He said, "The sacrifice that each one can make is to do his duty and obey my law. That is the form of penance I now demand." To be faithful to the duties of our state in life; to cling to God; to be faithful to His rule, His law, and His Church: That's what it means to be holy.

We need to understand that around us is a kind of shield, like a little cloud of wrinkly Saran wrap. We strain our eyes to look through all the things in the world that keep the vision of the truth from our eyes and keep the real goal of life from entering our hearts. We need to remember that we are a people of God who should know where we are and where we're going.

One of the questions people argue about when talking about Heaven is this: "Is Heaven a state, or is it a place?" By a state, I mean: Is it something within yourself—a frame of mind, an attitude of heart? Or is it a definite place?

Let's look at what Jesus said: "No one has gone up to heaven except the one who came down from heaven, the Son of Man who is in heaven" (John 3:13). It's important to understand this because it will tell us a lot about Heaven. The first part of Jesus' statement—"No one has gone up to Heaven except the one who came down"—tells us that Heaven is a definite place. But then He concludes with "the Son of Man who is in Heaven." We know that Jesus was both divine and human. He had one divine personality, but He had a human nature and a divine nature—two natures, one person. So the Lord, in His divinity, was always in Heaven, which means it is also a state.

So, Heaven is both a place and a state. It is something we can be in right now, where we are with God and God is in us. But it is also a place. When we die, our bodies stay here. They go back to the dust from which we were created. But our souls rise and are judged. The first thing you see when you die is Jesus.

Sometimes, as a meditation, I imagine myself on my deathbed. And suddenly, I feel my soul leaving my body. But you're not dead very long when the most glorious moment of life begins. The whole purpose of life, the whole purpose of God bringing us out of nothingness into this world, the whole purpose of our transforming journey comes to us face-to-face. We see God. We hear His voice.

What Is Heaven?

And immediately, I imagine, our whole life will pass before us — good, bad, and indifferent. But I think the most important thing that will happen is that we will want so much to run into His arms.

One time I was making prints of photos, and I had two negatives of the same layout. And the Lord said to me, "Angelica, do you see those negatives?" And I said, "Yes, Lord." He said, "Put them together." I put them together, and they were perfect: I couldn't see the least bit of difference between them; they looked like one negative. And He said, "That's Heaven. When you see Me face-to-face and My image in you is perfect at your death, you and I will be one."

Then He said to me, "Move the negative a little." The image became blurred because of the distortion. "That's an image of Purgatory," He told me. He was saying that, I realized, because I had said no to Him so many times that I wouldn't be able to see Him clearly or to go to Him, even though I would have nothing but the desire to be with Him because of His beauty, love, and compassion. That's Purgatory.

And then He said, "Separate them." I did, and each stood alone. He was saying to me, "That's hell, when a soul looks at Me at death and says, 'I don't love You,' and they turn away."

What Is Heaven?

Death is not so much a judgment as a revealing light. We, as Christians, must speak with great enthusiasm and great wonder about the Kingdom that is to come. The Kingdom of Heaven, after all, is within you; it is around you; it is above you. "No one has gone up to heaven except the one who came down from heaven, the Son of Man who is in heaven." (John 3:13) That's why it's so important to think of Heaven: we begin our Heaven, our Purgatory, or our Hell right here. We don't just plop from one state to another.

One of the reasons Heaven is so hard for us to understand is that, in Heaven, we will be loved by everyone in total unselfishness. Can you imagine being in a place or a family today where every member really and truly loved each other? If you do, then you live in Heaven here.

In today's culture, we talk an awful lot about love. I wonder, though, how much we really love. Would the world be in the condition it's in if we all loved everyone? If we all loved everybody on a human and divine level, we wouldn't have all the terrorism, prejudice, selfishness, robberies, murders, or anything else bad you can think of. We wouldn't be afraid. There would be no lying and cheating, no adultery, no lust.

You might say, "But that's impossible!" No! It's not impossible. Jesus made it possible. It's you and I who make it impossible.

What Is Heaven?

We might wonder, "What will we do in the Kingdom?" First, we'll just be loved by everybody! We won't have anybody going after us, hating us, or thinking we're in the way or useless. There will be no more loneliness in the Kingdom. We'll be able to speak to the most fantastic minds the world ever knew. We'll be able to interact with the angels, those glorious spirits! We'll be able to look at the Father face-to-face. We can't even imagine that kind of joy.

And we'll be free! There will be no more fear. No one on earth knows what it's like not to have fears. Everybody has them. In fact, today I think there's more fear in our society than in any other time. We fear everything and everyone. And often we're afraid even of ourselves. But in Heaven, that shackle will be torn away, and instead of experiencing fear and doubt — including all the doubts we've had about whether there's a God, why there's a God, why He does what He does — we shall see Him face-to-face.

St. Teresa of Avila had a vision of the hand of God. That's all she saw of Him. But she said that she would be willing to suffer all the pain in the world to the end of time just to see that hand once more. You and I have no comprehension of the majesty of God. Instead of just hoping for Him, in Heaven you and I will possess God.

We'll also never be discouraged again, and never tired. That will be terrific — never to feel fatigue, never to feel mentally drained. There will never be a mystery we can't understand. How are there three Persons in one God? And how did God make all of this? Those seemingly impossible questions will be answered. And we will never have to worry about our salvation again. We will know that we are in love with God and that God is in love with us and that everybody around us thinks we're the greatest.

We'll also know why everything happened in our lives. Boy, are we going to be embarrassed! If it were possible to be sorry in the Kingdom, we would be awfully sorry for having griped so much, for having questioned God's providence and mercy and will. We'll know why all the pains and tragedies happened in our life. It will become so clear that we'll look at God and say, "Thank You, Lord, for every time You said no to me."

Our Lord also said, "There are many rooms in my Father's house" (John 14:2). We're not all going to have the same degree of glory. Some people think that when we die and go to Heaven, everyone will be there like a herd of cattle, all in one place. But that's not the case.

Remember, we aren't equal in anything. We don't look alike; we don't have the same intelligence; we don't have the same talent; we don't have the same money; we don't have the same anything! So, in Heaven, there will be degrees of glory. St. Paul says that there will be some sent up with gold, precious stones, and diamonds, and others with wood or straw (see 1 Cor. 3:12–13).

There is so much disappointment in life: We've been disappointed by people, by ourselves, by society, by governments. But don't be afraid: Heaven will never disappoint you. When we get to Heaven, we will realize that, in spite of our weaknesses, there was glory in our everyday lives. In spite of all our pain and the imperfections, we will realize in the Kingdom that all of our weaknesses have somehow been bound up in our journey home.

Here's something that's very important for us to understand: You and I are no longer servants of God. Jesus said, "I shall not call you servants any more.... I call you friends" (John 15:15).

In the first days of Christianity, as the Christians lived their lives on their journey home, they proved the goodness of their faith by their purity. Purity is our knowledge of God, our patience, our kindness, our spirit of holiness, and our desire for the good. That's why it's so important that we make the right choices now. Don't listen to the world. Listen to the Word. Listen to the Church. Listen to your conscience. And make your choices in favor of the Lord.

Let us look at Our Lord and at ourselves without fear. God knows us, and He loves us as we are. More than that: He gives us the grace to be transformed. That's the most important thing in life. We don't just suddenly become a perfect saint who never loses her temper or never gives in to a temptation or never makes a mistake. That's a mummy; that's not a human being.

Jesus exhibited every kind of emotion: He cried; He sighed; He even was angry sometimes. He couldn't get over the incredulity of His apostles. He was hurt when people didn't give Him a kiss when He entered. So, everything that Jesus did, you and I do. We need to want to do it like Him. That is how we bring Heaven to earth—and how we prepare ourselves for the Kingdom to come.

Chapter 2

Heavenly Happiness

∞

It's very difficult to envision the joys of Heaven. On earth, everything feels so short-lived. We may be ecstatic one day, but the next day, nothing special happens and we find ourselves back to normal again. And so, it's difficult for us to imagine a place and a state where joy never ends.

You might ask how we know we can never lose joy in Heaven. Well, our experience of joy is always determined by things around us. In Heaven, we are surrounded by God, Who is the source of all joy and Who never changes. You and I have such abstract concepts of Heaven that we can't even imagine a never-ending Heaven.

On earth, everything ends. We get older. We can no longer do the things we used to do. Our friends and relatives come and go and move and die. They change; their feelings for you change; and your feelings for them change. This is life.

What Is Heaven?

Let's turn to the twenty-first chapter of the book of Revelation: "Then I heard a loud voice call from the throne, "You see this city? Here God lives among men" (Rev. 21:3). Can you imagine seeing the face of God? "He will make his home among them; they shall be his people, and he will be their God; his name is God-with-them" (Rev. 21:3). This next section is especially important for those who are lonely or who have lost someone very close: "He will wipe away all tears from their eyes; there will be no more death, and no more mourning or sadness" (Rev. 21:4). We can't even imagine what it would be like to be totally without those terrible feelings that so often come over us late at night and in the morning—those feelings of sadness, of mourning, of agitation.

Now, in this life, we cannot see God face-to-face. Scripture says that no one can see God and live (see Exod. 33:20). In a similar way, we cannot look directly at the sun, because our eyes were not made to look directly into that kind of power. Neither are our finite bodies and souls able to withstand the power of looking at God face-to-face. One of the great things God does for us when we enter the Kingdom is to give us this ability. Can you imagine the joy of that grace alone?

On earth, we're always fighting the good fight. Not five minutes go by during which we don't have to make some decision for good or for bad. But those in Heaven have won the good fight. What joy there is not just in having won but in being able to rest from the fight.

Our joy in Heaven will also be enhanced by the presence of our family and friends. God made us to be social beings; in Heaven, we won't just suddenly be individuals with no connections or particular loves. If we are social beings in this hectic, imperfect world, how much more will we be in Heaven? We will see and cherish our loved ones.

My grandfather always had a great devotion to Our Lady. In fact, if you said the name Mary, he would tip his hat or make a salute. Later in life, he became paralyzed, unable to move anything except his head. One day, my mother was in his room, changing pillowcases, and suddenly she saw two people near the door. She was petrified, as these two tall people just looked at my grandfather. One of them said, "Anthony," and my grandfather didn't respond. He said again, "Anthony," and this time my grandfather opened his eyes and sat up in bed! He looked at these two people, and two tears ran down his cheeks. All he said was "No," and he lay down again. But they just stood there and said again, "Anthony. Anthony!" Then he sat up again and looked at them as if suddenly he recognized them. And my mother said he smiled from ear to ear, and he nodded his head. He lay back in bed, and he died. God is so thoughtful; I'm sure that those whom you've loved and missed the most may come at your deathbed and say, "Come."

Everybody here on earth radiates God in a different way. In my community are many sisters, and we are all different. We don't have the same talents, the same temperaments, or the same tastes. We don't have the same degree of intelligence or education. We don't even pray alike.

So, there is just no way we're all going to be alike in the Kingdom. A person who has suffered much or who has been deprived here on earth stores up great treasures in Heaven. And there are those who spend their whole lives loving God and doing His Will. And then there are those who don't know God and really don't care about Him for most of their earthly lives, but, by some special grace, five seconds before they die, they say, "Lord, I'm sorry." And they're saved. There's all kinds of people and all kinds of ways of knowing God and loving God. This will still be so in Heaven, where we will each see God in a different way. While everyone in Heaven has complete access to the truth of God, each one understands the mysteries of God in a different way.

This relates to the mystery of pain and suffering in this life and the way our reality in Heaven will reflect our experience on earth. Look at the parable about the rich man and Lazarus (Luke 16:19–31). The rich man had everything he needed, while Lazarus the leper had his sores licked by stray dogs. But when they both died, the Lord said that Lazarus was taken to the bosom of Abraham, while the rich man, who depended entirely on his wealth and not upon God, was sent to Hades. This doesn't mean that all the wealthy go down and the poor go up, but it teaches us that it doesn't depend on what you have or don't have here on earth. Our ultimate fate depends on the amount of love that we have for God when He says to us, "Come."

Another thing we have to understand is that the joy of Heaven is always going to be fresh. There will always be something new to be joyful about. In Heaven, because God is infinite, there is no end to the things we can learn about Him. He will be forever new to us.

We will also have no memories that haunt us. This is another reason we often have a hard time thinking of Heaven, because we think we're going to be remorseful, forever looking at the sins and mistakes of our past. But that will all be gone. There will be no painful memories or guilt. Jesus says, "There will be more rejoicing in Heaven over one repentant sinner than over ninety-nine virtuous"(Luke 15:7). How can we have more joy in Heaven? Our capacity for love doesn't change in the Kingdom, but we feel a special glory over one sinner who repents.

What Is Heaven?

We're not accustomed in life to being loved so much. It's a great gift from God when we find people who love us for ourselves. But people change, and so our joys in life grow and shrink. In fact, they depend a lot on whether someone loves us or doesn't love us. You go to work one day, and your boss smiles at you because he's in a great mood—and you feel great. And then the next day, he's grouchy—and so are you. And so our life is like a seesaw. But the closer we get to the Lord, the more Jesus is in us in our daily lives, and the more we see God in the present moment, the more serenity we feel and the fewer ups and downs we experience.

We're expected to begin our Heaven here in this life. It doesn't matter what state of life we are in: There is no excuse. We are children of God; we were created by God; we were placed on this earth in this place and this age; and we are called to be holy.

The beautiful thing about Christianity is that it gives us the faith to see God as He really is—in this life. Joy must begin here. When we begin to see God in the present moment—even though the present moment may hurt us and may sometimes even devastate us—we can still have that assurance that God's providence is at work. What we see in faith here on earth, we will see in reality in the Kingdom.

And, of course, there's a tremendous difference between the two. It's like looking at a recipe for pie and then eating a piece of the pie. When we're reading the recipe, we have to use our imagination. We have faith in the recipe. Well, if we can have faith in *that*, we can have faith in God!

Hope in this life is looking forward to the promises of God. But Heaven is the possession of those promises. When we pray, sometimes we wonder if God hears us. He does hear, of course, but we still wonder. But in Heaven, we can just go right up to the Father, and we'll see Him and He'll see us, and we'll talk to Him. So, joy is perfected in Heaven, but we must begin to possess it now.

Joy, after all, is a sign of a Christian. The pagans in the first century were drawn to Christians' joy and the way they loved one another. It's hard to love and be loved by a sourpuss. We have to have smiles on our faces and love in our eyes. The early Christians had some pretty heavy crosses — such as the possibility of being thrown to the lions, or losing their homes and all their possessions, or having to escape to other countries and hide underground. But they had that visible sign of Christ about them, so much so that if a soldier walked up to them on the street, he could immediately pick them out. Don't you wonder if they could pick us out today? Don't you wonder if they could identify that joy, that sign of God's presence dwelling in us?

What Is Heaven?

Let's look at John's Gospel: "Remain in my love. If you keep my commandments you will remain in my love, just as I have kept my Father's commandments and remain in his love. I have told you this so that my own joy may be in you and your joy be complete" (John 15:9–11). How can we have complete joy in this life, which seems to tear us down all the time? The only way is to see the Will of God in everything and to make every effort to be like Jesus.

We Christians can afford to be joyful because we know that Christ has risen. Jesus says, "You are sad now, but I shall see you again, and your hearts will be full of joy, and that joy no one shall take from you" (John 16:22). No one! This is a promise of Jesus, and Jesus is true to His promises.

You know, we could be loved by ten thousand people, but if one person hates us, our happiness is marred. We could be in a room where everyone loves us, but if one person who can't stand us walks in, our enjoyment of that gathering is suddenly gone. If we see God's Will around us, our pervading joy won't leave us—though the passing feeling of happiness might. In the Kingdom, though, joy and happiness go together, and nothing can take away either one.

In St. Luke's Gospel, Jesus delivers this Beatitude: "Happy are you when people hate you, drive you out, abuse you, denounce your name as criminal, on account of the Son of

Man" (Luke 6:22). We might ask, "What am I supposed to do about it, Lord? Shall I run? Shall I hide? Shall I change?" But the Lord says, "Rejoice when that day comes and dance for joy, then your reward will be great in heaven" (Luke 6:23).

Our Lord is terribly demanding. If we try to live this Gospel and we find it easy, then we're not living it. But the truth is that our suffering makes sense even in the here and now. Suffering is the greatest scandal in the world today. We keep hiding it. We take Jesus off the Cross. We don't understand suffering at all. But Luke 6:23 tells us how we should react to suffering.

In the first chapter of Colossians, St. Paul talks about the saints. They "inherit the light." (Col. 1:12). "It makes me happy to suffer for you, as I am suffering now" (Col. 1:24). There it is right there: "happy." Paul understood. Joy is the mark of a Christian because, though in life we live by faith, we live in hope of what is to come and in love of God and our neighbor.

St. Peter says in his first letter, "My dear people, you must not think it unaccountable that you should be tested by fire. There is nothing extraordinary in what has happened to you. If you can have some share in the sufferings of Christ, be glad, because you will enjoy a much greater gladness when his glory is revealed" (1 Pet. 4:12–14). The joy that is to come must begin to take shape right here.

What Is Heaven?

This is the mark of hope, the mark of faith, and the mark of love — the mark that Jesus has put upon us because God is our source of joy in Heaven and, as we overcome so many things, here on earth.

Chapter 3

The Work of the Saints

∞

Let's talk about work in Heaven. You might think, "I worked all my life! I don't want to work in Heaven!" And this question of what we will do in Heaven really has puzzled millions of people for centuries. We can start here: A place of happiness cannot be a place of idleness. We can't be happy and be idle because, in a sense, we disintegrate: Here on earth, our muscles disintegrate, and, in a broader sense, our nature disintegrates. Remember that even Adam and Eve worked in the Garden of Eden. So, since Heaven, like the Garden, is a place of total happiness, common sense tells us that there must be some kind of work in Heaven.

The very first chapter of Genesis talks about God's work —how He worked for six days and rested on the seventh. Let's just imagine God in His Heaven before He created you and me, when there wasn't anything but God. There were no angels, no men, no trees, no flowers, nothing except the Trinity—Father, Son, and Holy Spirit. God had to create everything—and that was a lot of work! We must remember that everything has been created by God. He worked to create mountains and skies and air and water and animals and vegetables and fruits.

And God's work continues. Jesus said, "My food is to do the will of the one who sent me, and to complete his work" (John 4:34). Our trouble is that we don't have any concept of work except as something that takes exertion and creates fatigue. We have lost the joy and the creativity of work because, for most of us, it's drudgery. The only thing that changes in the Kingdom is the kind of work.

Why do we work here? We work to eat, to sleep, to pay our rent, to pay our bills. We work to maintain our houses, to keep our families and our bodies going. But in Scripture we see a different concept of work, because in Heaven there is no need to make a living or to eat or to sleep. That kind of work will be unnecessary. But there are other kinds of work: "The works my Father has given me to carry out, these same works of mine testify that the Father has sent me" (John 5:36).

And when we look at the life of Jesus, it becomes clear that the greatest work Jesus undertook was our sanctification. Even before He healed people physically, He healed their souls. He would forgive their sins, or He would call for faith and humility before He healed their bodies. This was His greatest work. And this is why we get so mixed up when we talk about work in Heaven. We will no longer have to work to sustain the body, because that kind of life will be over. But we will do the work of the soul.

The greatest work is not the kind that changes things but the kind that changes people. The greatest work we will have, even in this life, is not our career or other worldly accomplishments, but our sanctification—and that of our friends and family and everyone else in our lives. Have we given ourselves over to the Will of God so we can be holy as He is holy? That's the really hard work, because we have to take ourselves in our hands and take control. We have to be gentle when we don't feel gentle; we have to repent when we feel angry. If we don't think that's work, then we haven't worked.

In the book of Daniel, an angel appears to Daniel and says, "Daniel, do not be afraid: from that first day when you resolved to humble yourself before God, the better to understand, your words have been heard." And he says, "And your words are the reason why I have come" (Dan. 10:12). This is an angel of the Lord, who is in the same Kingdom you will be in and who is doing the same things you will do. Visiting earth to address God's people is one of the works of Heaven. St. Thomas Aquinas said that all the galaxies of God's universe are governed by the angels to keep them on their course. Scientists may laugh at this, but that's because we tend to forget that God is not just sitting around up there doing nothing. When our bodies are united once more with our souls at the general resurrection, we're going to have to do a lot of things together.

We might think that we don't want to do only spiritual works in Heaven. But can we really think of anything better? Is our earthly work that much better? We work all week, and then half of what we earn goes to the government. As for me, I think I'd settle for what's up in Heaven.

One of those spiritual works in the Kingdom will be to pray for those still on earth. We might think that doesn't sound very hard, but let's think about it for a minute. Imagine that you're in Heaven and someone you love very dearly is down here on earth making mistakes and going in the wrong direction, away from Christ. You're going to pray hard for them, and that's going to be your work, to try to move them in the right direction. I'm sure that God will give us permission to direct the ways of those we love when we're in Heaven. Many times, I'm sure, we have been saved by friends and family members who have gone before us. We will be up there fighting against the enemies of God, not with the weapons of war that destroy but with the weapons of goodness and compassion and love.

When people we love die, it can be difficult for us to think they still know and understand and care about us. But they do, just as we will know and understand and care about our loved ones on earth after we die! If they cared for us in this imperfect earthly state, they do so all the more now in a perfect state! They have even more power now to inspire us.

In this world, I find spiritual work much more fatiguing than physical work. When we finish some physical work, it's finished for good. But spiritual work is never finished. The hardest work I do is trying to get other people to understand the depth of their being and spirituality so that they can rise above the mundane. But in Heaven, there will be no fatigue; we can go about that work continuously without worry or tiredness. Our work in Heaven will be tremendous, because we will be dealing with souls. And only God knows what other things we will be assigned.

My parents divorced when I was a young child. Six months before he died, my father told me that he was sorry about everything, but I still worried about him a lot. The first thing I did when I heard he was dead was to call the hospital to make sure he had received the last sacraments. Well, when my mother was dying, she looked toward the door and saw my father — the man she couldn't live with (nor he with her, apparently), the man I saw very little of in my life, the man who left one day and never came back — who had come back for the bride he couldn't keep on earth, the woman he thought he didn't love. I thought it was an amazing grace! My mother said, "But he looked so handsome and so beautiful." I wonder if that was his work as a kind of reparation for leaving her alone so many years ago. I wonder if it was his assignment from God to take care of her after death since he neglected her in life.

We often feel very lonely when we lose someone we love. But they're working for us — not with hands and feet, as we remember them, but they're working. They're trying to direct us, to comfort us, to give us hope, to make us understand in some way that there is something greater ahead. And I'm sure that, if they could weep, they would do so when they see us going after the wrong things.

It doesn't matter what we have or don't have here on earth. The work of everyday living is important work, but it's not the most important work we are called to. Our greatest work on earth is to cooperate with the Will of God in the present moment so that the Spirit of the Lord can transform us into His image. If we miss that, no matter how hard we might work on our careers or other things, we've lost everything!

Everything is going to pass except that main spiritual work, and that work will carry over into the Kingdom. We won't sit there disinterested in our loved ones or in mankind. If the angels rejoice over that one sinner, they must know the sinner: they must know what he has done; and they must have been praying for him in order to rejoice. If that's true of the angels, how much more true is it of glorified humans, who knew so many people while living on this earth?

You know, we get so tired on earth. Sometimes we feel as if we don't even look forward to continuing on. But we say that only because we're tired of what we're doing. We would never get tired of something that made us ecstatically happy. When we doubt that our loved ones are helping us from Heaven, we're judging the glory of the Kingdom by the standards of a body that's getting weaker after years of earthly labor. But this body is going to go. We can't compare the physical and the spiritual.

A lot of people are afraid to go to Heaven because they're ashamed of their actions and they're afraid that everybody up there is going to know exactly what they did wrong. But we can't think that way. Every time we go to Confession, the Lord forgives *and* forgets. Everybody has a skeleton in a closet. Do you think Heaven is a place where God parades around everybody's skeletons? That's not the God we know and love. "Though your sins are like scarlet, they shall be as white as snow" (Isa. 1:18).

It's very important to understand that everything we do, even the sins we commit, God will bring up for our good. You and I are created by God and have been placed in a testing ground — that's what life is, a big testing ground — to prepare us for a place in the Kingdom. That's why we were created: to cooperate with God.

It is very important that you arrive in His Kingdom. If you should turn away from God at the moment of death and have the terrible misfortune of losing your soul, your place in the Kingdom will never be filled by anyone else for all eternity. It's not like a big party where, if one person is missing, somebody else takes his place. Your place in the Kingdom will be empty forever unless you occupy it.

Preparing to take our place in the Kingdom is the greatest and most difficult work on earth. But then we will continue that most glorious work of all — praising God, enjoying the beauty of His Kingdom, praying for those who are still outside of it, loving those we loved on earth, directing them, interceding for them—all in a place of perfect joy and perfect happiness, with power we never had on earth. That is our work in Heaven, the greatest work of all.

Chapter 4

∞

Friends and Family in Heaven

In Heaven, we're going to have ideal friendships with everyone. This is why Jesus gave us the great commandment to love one another in the way He loves us, because that's how we're going to love in Heaven. And this is why He asks us to forgive our enemies, because there's a chance we're going to live with that enemy in love and friendship forever. So we have to start here.

We've talked about this before, but it bears repeating: Your Heaven, your Purgatory, and your Hell start right here. Every single aspect of these states of being begins on earth: Right now we are experiencing Heaven, Hell, or Purgatory. A lot of this has to do with our relationships.

Let's think about what friendship means. Most people have a best friend—or, if we're lucky, more than one friend—whose shoulder we can cry on and who accepts us as we are, with all our faults and failings and imperfections.

What Is Heaven?

This is the kind of friend who genuinely loves us — that is, who wants the very best for us, our sanctification and salvation, and who helps us along the way. Friends love God together. Now, imagine the very best version of that kind of friendship, without having to put up with all the imperfections and all the misunderstandings of our fallen world, and you can imagine how everyone in Heaven will be.

But what about enemies — the people we feel we have every reason to hate and not to forgive? Well, if we follow the Lord's commandment and forgive an enemy, and that person makes all the right choices and gets to Heaven, he will thank you for all eternity for your mercy and compassion, which helped him get there. The thing is, if we refuse to forgive someone we think is a bad guy, we might find out in the end that he made it and we didn't. The poor man may have been sorry, not even knowing he hurt you that bad, and because of his contrition, he spends eternity singing the praises of God while you spend eternity separated from Him! That's why Our Lord insists that we forgive and let Him take care of the rest. We must love as He loves and forgive as He forgives. When we hate and refuse to forgive, we are already living in a kind of Hell.

Now, in Heaven, our friendship is not going to be determined by our social status. We might claim that our friendships here aren't related to social status, but let's be honest. We all, at some point, form relationships in order to climb that ladder. We like to be seen with rich and famous and powerful people—even if just in our little worlds. When I was in high school, I had a hard time. I used to envy all those kids in the Honor Society. And I remember trying to make friends with the girl who was president of the Honor Society. She looked down on me and said, "Who are you?" And I said, "Nobody."

We all do these crazy things in our lives: We run after those who are smarter than we are, or who have more education or social status. We waste a lot of time trying to get into the "right" circles. This means that at least some of our friendships are a little bit false and some are very selfish. But in Heaven, all those complications will be gone. We will not all have the same degree of glory in Heaven, but we'll all be equally happy with each other and with God.

Our friendship in Heaven is going to be sincere and secure. We will see each other in God, and God in each other. We don't do that today. When we look at a neighbor or co-worker, we see only a veneer. We see all the imperfections and all the little temper tantrums and all the impatience and all the sensitivities, and they grind on us. We never get deep inside anyone. We might love (or not love) what we think is there, but we don't know what's really there.

What Is Heaven?

Many centuries ago, a religious brother who had a great reputation for holiness died, and a prostitute died on the same day. And they dumped the prostitute in a grave and forgot about her, whereas, amid much adulation and praise, they buried the brother. That night, the abbot had a vision. The brother was in Purgatory, and he was going to be there for a long time being purified of his many sins. But the prostitute went straight to Heaven. The prostitute had been genuinely sorry for the life she led—not out of fear of punishment, but only because she had offended God so much. She made a perfect act of love for God. But the brother's holiness was only skin deep; he did many things just to be seen by men. That's why Our Lord tells us not to judge.

In Heaven, every talent and every virtue that we have will be seen and enjoyed with no jealousy. In fact, we will be able to tell by how we look and what we wear exactly what virtues we excelled in, because everything about our appearance will have meaning. And the most marvelous thing will be that, as we look around, we will see people we've wondered and worried about, and we will see how God brought good out of everything. Right now, we see only the surface, and we get angry—with our friends, with our family, with ourselves, and with God.

At the Transfiguration, Jesus' "clothes became dazzlingly white, whiter than any earthly bleacher could make them"

(Mark 9:3). Later in the Gospel of Mark, when people challenge Jesus' teaching about the resurrection, He replies, "Is not the reason why you go wrong, that you understand neither the scriptures nor the power of God?" (Mark 12:24). I wonder today if we really understand the Scriptures or the power of God. We limit God. We have little, itty-bitty gods that we make in our image. But we are made in *His* image. He is Lord; He is sovereign. We must listen to and obey the sovereign Lord.

Jesus told the people, "For when they rise from the dead, men and women do not marry; no, they are like the angels in heaven" (Mark 12:25). This is a whole new kind of life. We can look further ahead to the book of Revelation: "Those who prove victorious will be dressed, like these, in white robes; I shall not blot their names out of the book of life, but acknowledge their names in the presence of my Father and his angels" (Rev. 3:5). Imagine yourself in this fantastic garment, approaching the throne of God with Jesus at your side. And He says your name, and it rings through Heaven with power, and the angels rejoice. It's like a big celebration after a general comes home from victory, but this was the war against evil. You made it.

Later in the book of Revelation, we read again about people clothed in white robes; this time it specifies that these are people who suffered great persecution on earth (Rev. 7:9,

14). Chapter 14 says that white-robed people are in front of the throne: "They were singing a new hymn ..., a hymn that could only be learned by the hundred and forty-four thousand who had been redeemed from the world" (Rev. 14:3). That number is an expression, a symbol of potentially millions and millions of people. "These are the ones who have kept their virginity and not been defiled" (Rev. 14:4). Finally, in the nineteenth chapter: "The reign of the Lord our God Almighty has begun; let us be glad and joyful and give praise to God, because this is the time for the marriage of the Lamb. His bride is ready, and she has been able to dress herself in dazzling white linen, because her linen is made of the good deeds of the saints" (Rev. 19:7–9).

Now, what happens in Heaven if someone we loved on earth isn't there? We might think that we couldn't possibly be happy. But there is nothing in Heaven that can mar our happiness. In Heaven, we will see the full reality of the people we loved on earth—and of those we didn't. We will see that, down deep in the hearts of some people whom we thought were wonderful, there may have been terrible evil and rejection of God. Although it is hard to think about this now, we will not be less happy in Heaven if someone we knew and loved is not there. This is because we will love as God loves, and we will know that that person, on his own, with his own free will, turned away and said, "I don't want to be with You. I don't want to be in Your Kingdom."

This can be hard for us to take, especially when we think about people we love very deeply. But these are questions that we must face here — the question of whether we are seeing the whole person, and the question of whether we are choosing for God ourselves. In Heaven, our love for others, whether they are with us or not, will not disappear; it will be purified. Our love will be pure in Heaven, because we will love with the same pure love that God loves with.

We will never suffer betrayal in Heaven. It's the worst pain in the world to love someone for a long time and then suddenly to find out that that person didn't love us at all. But in Heaven, everyone's love is based on God, who is unchanging. And that's why the new commandment to love one another is so important on earth, because we have to begin our Heaven here. We must be an image of the unchanging Jesus to everyone.

Many people wonder whether we will know our family members in Heaven. Of course we will! The memory is part of the soul. Our brains die, but our souls live on. In fact, our memory will be enhanced in Heaven. We won't remember all our sins and weaknesses, but we will remember people.

Now, the people we see in Heaven might look different than they do now. My opinion, which has nothing to do with theology or revelation or anything, is that everybody in Heaven is going to look like the Lord at the age of thirty-three (the age at which He died)—that is, as a young adult. If a baby dies, I don't think he'll be a baby in Heaven. Think of all the women who have had miscarriages, or who have had abortions and are very repentant and sorry: It may be that they will see their babies in Heaven as they would have been as young adults on earth, all grown up. And the parents and grandparents we've lost at an old age, all wrinkly and bent over—we'll know them immediately in Heaven, but they might not look just as we remember them.

All the relationships that were broken on earth, such as those between parents and their estranged children, will be healed in Heaven—provided everyone has responded to the grace to repent and apologize and be purified. You'll see each other again, and all the coldness and loneliness will be gone. This is why we need to have hope. When parents see their children going down deeper and deeper into sin and despair, they must never lose trust in God. Don't ever stop praying: One prayer can do wondrous things. In Heaven, we'll know why God permitted all these things that worried us, and we'll know the fruits of our prayers.

It's true that we can never really imagine Heaven. We can talk about it, as we have been, based on the words of

Scripture and the words of the saints, but our mind can't comprehend the fullness of it. But that doesn't mean we should stop thinking about it—not at all! How could we read the Bible and think that we should just ignore Heaven? Think about what happened to Jesus. He was scourged and crowned with thorns. How the blood must have run down His cheeks! He carried His Cross, falling multiple times on His face. He looked at His mother in that pitiful condition. He was nailed to the wood. Surgeons say that when they hung up the arms of the condemned, it hit a nerve that is so painful, it could make you go mad. Why would the Son of God, the Eternal Word, the Image of the Father, go through all of that? For what? For Heaven! That's how incredible Heaven is!

How can we not desire Heaven? Well, partly because we never think about it. We misuse Paul's magnificent verse about not hearing or seeing or knowing the glory of Heaven (1 Cor. 2:9) and just blot it out of our minds. As a result, we're afraid to die; we have no concept of why we suffer on earth; and we have no concept of what is going to come. We live in the darkness. But God gave us enough information to desire to be there with Him.

We have to think of Heaven. Why did the first Christians sing songs when they saw those huge lions coming after them? They weren't all saved from the beasts: They were chewed up in front of thousands of cheering people. How could St. Stephen calmly look up and say that he saw the Son of God on the right hand of the Father while being stoned to death (Acts 7:55–56)? Because they all looked forward to Heaven!

So, how can we bear our crosses? How can we bear the loneliness of an empty house if we don't know there is a wonderful Heaven waiting for us? How can we bear each day of fear and peril? How can we watch the news and not have that hope of something better to come? How can we bear that burden of constant pain without hope for Heaven? We must have that hope and faith, just as Jesus and the first Christians did. I firmly believe that some of us will miss out on Heaven not so much for our sins as for our lack of appreciation for what He did for us — that is, our lack of desire for Heaven. To be in that place where we can no longer offend God; to be in that place where we never have to worry about whether we're going to make it or not; to be in that place where we can see those we loved and those we didn't love with equal love; to see the wonders of the Kingdom: It would be wrong not to want that more than anything.

Are we under the impression that this tiny dot in the middle of the universe is the only beauty God ever made? That can't be! It doesn't make sense! And it's all passing — the waterfalls and the mountains, the smile of a child, the beauty and wisdom of age, the glory of a sunrise, the quiet of a sunset, the exhilaration of a rainbow after a good, hard rain, the beauty of lightning and the softness of snow, the power of the wind and the gentleness of a breeze. Do we imagine that that's all there is? It's as if the Lord passed by and the fringe of His garment touched the earth, and suddenly there were trees and fruit and people and mountains and hills—and the most important thing, love. But that's nothing compared with what is to come.

Chapter 5

∽∞∽

The Music and Beauty of Heaven

∞

Now we're going to talk about music and beauty in Heaven.

When we speak about Heaven there is a tendency to dismiss our speculation as "just imagining things." But Our Dear Lord, knowing that we need examples that are a little more concrete, gives us ever-so-tiny hints of Heaven—lights and ideas and experiences that are going to be very similar, only greatly enhanced in Heaven.

Let's take music. There are all kinds of music, and each one of our hearts rejoices in some kind of music. Some like classical; some like rock; some like jazz; and so on. But we don't hear the same thing, even when we like the same kind of music. So, let's go through some of the kinds of music we experience in life—some that we hear with our ears, and some that stirs our souls even if we aren't listening. All of these will be present, but perfected, in Heaven.

What Is Heaven?

When we think of music, we tend to think mostly of music played on instruments. But there's much more to it than that. For example, have you ever realized that there is a music of nature, ringing out the creative powers of God? Have you gone into the woods lately? If you say you're too busy, you're missing out on half of life — going out into nature and listening to the breeze and to the music. Nature has a tune! Listen to the music of the branches as they rustle in the wind. Listen to the crackling of leaves under your feet. Listen to water fall down a hillside. We might say that's just noise, but no: It's just a different kind of music. I love to go to the ocean and just stand there and feel and hear the waves as they go *whoosh*. They sound so quiet but so powerful. That's music. We don't hear it because we're so busy between our ears.

And then, of course, there is the music of instruments. When our sisters here at the monastery are practicing for Mass, sometimes I don't even join them: I just like to sit there and listen. It's a kind of recreation for me. They play with love, and even their mistakes are beautiful to me. The music of instruments enlivens the emotions. Sometimes when they're playing something very beautiful, I look up at the Blessed Sacrament, and all I can do is say, "Jesus, You're so wonderful. I love You." Musical instruments can take our emotions and raise them up to God.

Then there's the music of silence. Silence is more than the absence of noise: You can have an absence of noise and not even hear the music of silence. I'm talking about the music of silence that is quiet, but filled with His thunderous presence. We can all just take a half a second to listen to the silence in the room and see if there isn't a kind of thunderous, awesome presence. That's not really absence of noise: It's the omnipresent God—and it's a tiny hint of what we're going to feel and understand in the Kingdom.

Now, here on earth there's also what I like to call the music of pain. This music of pain is a little offbeat. One time, when I was a young novice, we were practicing a song I thought might have been the worst song anybody ever wrote. It seemed totally out of key, as if no one was singing harmoniously with anyone else. But after many days of practice, it suddenly became absolutely beautiful. I asked the music director what kind of music it was, and she told me it was polyphony. It still sounded offbeat, but I recognized this beauty in it. That, to me, is the beautiful music of pain. I think that, in the eyes of God, of the Kingdom, and of the ones you love and miss, that kind of offbeat music is your pain ascending to God; it's a hymn of resignation to God's Will. I think it is perhaps the kind of beautiful music that Jesus sang on the Cross.

What Is Heaven?

And then there is the music that comes from loneliness. Have you ever emptied a glass and then tapped it with a fork or knife or something and the tone it produced was absolutely phenomenal? I think the music that you sing to God by the emptying of your vessel — by the accomplishment of the Will of God in your life — pierces the Heavens.

There's also the music of the heart — a music that can't be expressed in words or even tones. Imagine two people who love each other sitting together and quietly holding hands: Even though they aren't saying anything, their hearts are singing. You can see it in their faces, because love is a melody that cheers the heart. We can imagine a time when we were wonderfully content for a few hours or a few days, maybe on a trip or while visiting with loved ones or while on a walk in the woods, and there's a feeling of joy that is a real song — different from what we can verbalize, different from the notes on the scale, but nonetheless a kind of music.

And then there is what I call the music of light, which shines on the soul that's reaching out to find and understand its Creator. It's the light on the face of a child who is unsullied by the world, who innocently looks up in wonder and awe. That certainly brings out music in the heart.

We can also think of the music of accomplishment, of a job well done, of having the grace from God to overcome a terrible weakness. Remember what the Lord said: "There will be more rejoicing in heaven over one repentant sinner than over ninety-nine virtuous men who have no need of repentance" (Luke 15:7); we cannot rejoice without song. And finally, there is the music of friendship, which lightens our burdens and makes our hearts bubble over with the joy of love. This is another music that we hear with the heart.

So, most of the music that is a foretaste of Heaven is not made by instruments, but it is nonetheless music. All these kinds of music make up a symphony of our lives. A symphony is made up of movements; some of these movements during our lives are heavy, dark, and thunderous, and others are light and joyous. The last movement of our lives, however, is the best. Throughout our lives, there are a lot of sour notes and ugly harmonies. But that last movement that is in Heaven is perfect.

And one of the beautiful things is that all of Heaven will listen as you strum your own hymn of praise. All the angels will stop; all the saints will stand still as you go into the Kingdom for the first time. In Psalm 8 it says, "Above the heavens is your majesty chanted by the mouths of children, babes in arms" (Ps. 8:1–2). And for all of us who have lost loved ones, let's turn to Psalm 30: "You have turned my mourning into dancing, you have stripped off my sackcloth" (Ps. 30:11). We all wear sackcloth today: all our mistakes, sins, imperfections, and frailties. "You have stripped off my sackcloth and wrapped me in gladness; and now my heart, silent no longer, will play you music; Yahweh, my God, I will praise you for ever" (Ps. 30:11–12).

Let's look again at the book of Revelation, where there is amazing imagery about music (and silence) in the Kingdom. In Revelation 15, we read about the beautiful melody of the angels and saints: "They all had harps from God, and they were singing the hymn of Moses, the servant of God, and of the Lamb" (Rev. 15:2–3). But in the eighth chapter we read, "The Lamb then broke the seventh seal, and there was silence in heaven for about half an hour" (Rev. 8:1). The majesty of God had become so glorious in the entire Kingdom there was nothing but quiet awe. And then, suddenly all the Kingdom began to sing, "Alleluia! Victory and glory and power to our God!" (Rev. 19:1).

Even those of us who don't care for music very much will be exhilarated. Every bit of imperfection will be gone. It makes me think of the angels who appeared to the shepherds at Jesus' birth and announced the good news in song: "Glory to God. The Messiah is here." The first Christians sang all the time, sometimes even as they were in the arena waiting to be devoured by lions. Can you imagine what a beautiful song that must have been to God? And can you imagine the effect it must have had on the people in the arena who were crying out for their blood? This was a song of abandonment to the Will of God, the song of total freedom, free of fear of anyone or anything. When we think of that kind of song, don't we wish we could sing it right now?

After all, in the fifth chapter of Ephesians, St. Paul says, "Sing the words and tunes of the psalms and hymns when you are together, and go on singing and chanting to the Lord in your hearts" (Eph. 5:19). That's how we'll pray in the Kingdom, with a song coming from our hearts. You see, in Heaven, we will sing tunes in our hearts and minds because we will see everlasting beauty face-to-face. There will be nothing we can say. We have no more concept of the beauty of God than a child in the womb has a concept of the beauty of his mother's face or a sunrise or a sunset. As we begin to sing in the Kingdom, we will sing of His mercy to us. We will understand how many times He protected us, guarded us, guided us, and how many times He kept us from even greater sins than the ones we committed, even greater mistakes than the ones we made.

Here on earth, parents can pick out the voices of their children and understand them even when no one else can. Well, in the Kingdom, God will hear and understand us as if no one else existed.

What Is Heaven?

I want to talk now about those who have especially suffered or struggled here on earth. Can you imagine, for instance, the songs that the deaf will hear and sing? Those songs will be even more beautiful than the ones most of us hear and sing. That's because God is just, so those who have been deprived here, whether through poverty or accident or heredity or mistakes or sin, if they have repented, will be blessed in abundance in Heaven. If someone has been born blind, he will see things most of us won't see. Those who are intellectually disabled will understand mysteries of God that most of us will never understand. St. Paul says, "I think that what we suffer in this life can never be compared to the glory, as yet unrevealed, which is waiting for us" (Rom. 8:18).

Some of us might worry about what we'll miss in Heaven because we've been blessed with good health and good fortune here on earth. Well, we don't need to worry, because we will also have things that others will not have. Our happiness in the Kingdom will be overflowing because each one of us will have experiences that no one else will have — because our sufferings were so different, because our anxieties were so different, because our personalities and temperaments were so different. This isn't a kind of punishment. There's no punishment in the Kingdom. It's simply a matter of justice.

So those of us who have seen and heard and spoke and smelled and tasted all our lives will have different glories and different joys in Heaven. But we will all share the greatest joy of all, rejoicing that we have been called by God through the Precious Blood of Jesus to be glorious in His Kingdom.

Let's conclude by looking at the description of Heaven in Revelation 21. "The angel that was speaking to me was carrying a gold measuring rod.... The city is perfectly square, its length the same as its breadth. He measured the city with his rod and it was twelve thousand furlongs in length and in breadth" (Rev. 21:15–16). We might think we have some pretty nice diamonds in our rings, but the biggest diamonds on earth are pebbles compared with those in Heaven. "The wall was built of diamond, and the city of pure gold, like polished glass" (Rev. 21:18–19). We're talking about big hunks of precious stones, not these little things you see in jewelers' cases. "The twelve gates were twelve pearls" (Rev. 21:21). One pearl a piece! It makes it look as if we're playing with toys in this world. Isn't it a shame that we get so attached to them?

The description goes on, with floors of golden glass and no darkness, since the light of God never goes out (Rev. 21:21, 23). You might think this is all symbolic, but how can you say? I know that there are many ways of reading

What Is Heaven?

Scripture, and you can read the same passage in all three ways—mystical, literal, symbolic—but no matter how you slice it, you'll never be able to prove exactly what it's like. But it will certainly be absolutely incredible.

Why are we afraid to transform ourselves in this life, to accept the cross as it comes to us day after day, hour after hour, minute after minute, if we can look forward to what is to come? I think the most glorious moment in the Kingdom will be when God looks at us and we look at Him face-to-face for the first time. And He will look at us with such love that, were it not for a special grace, we would melt away into nothingness. For the look of God is so powerful and so beautiful and so loving that it makes our entire earthly lives seem like nothing.

Chapter 6

∞

Knowledge in Heaven

∞

I am thrilled every time the Lord gives me insight into some new concept about the Kingdom. Take a look at First Corinthians 13:11, and you will find something interesting: "When I was a child, I used to talk like a child, and think like a child, and argue like a child" (1 Cor. 13:11). St. Paul's temperament comes up every so often in his letters; everyone who has a hot temper should have St. Paul as a favorite saint. That's why he's my favorite saint: I like people who had tempers, who had hard struggles to overcome themselves.

Then St. Paul writes, "Now we are seeing a dim reflection in a mirror" (1 Cor. 13:12). Everything we see of God today, in nature, in our fellow human beings, in our intellects, is like an image in a dim mirror. We all have either seen or can imagine an old dusty mirror—maybe found in an attic. The reflection is there, but it's not too hot! All of creation, all its beauty, is like a dim mirror. St. Paul continues, now talking about Heaven, "But then we shall be seeing face-to-face" (1 Cor. 13:12). I can't imagine the moment, that marvelous moment that we call death, when we will see God face-to-face. "The knowledge that I have now is imperfect; but then I shall know as fully as I am known" (1 Cor. 13:12). That knowledge is the topic of this section.

One of the most delightful experiences in Heaven is going to be the acquisition of knowledge. Now, back in school, I worked very hard for my Fs. It's true! I had so many problems at home, and I was hungry most of the time, so I couldn't study. I wasn't interested in the capital of Iowa! But in Heaven it's going to be very different! We won't be hampered by laborious methods of learning. We won't need books and instructors and lectures. In Heaven, our intellects will connect directly with God. And our memories will no longer struggle to recall truths. One of the most marvelous things in the Kingdom is that we will know truth clearly. It will all be clear as a bell. Whatever truth God wishes us to know, we'll know it immediately.

We're going to know about God, of course, but we're also going to know about ourselves—perfectly. Pope John XXIII had a sign on his desk that just said, "Know yourself."

A lot of our problems are due to the fact that we don't know ourselves. The image I have of myself is not the image that others have of me. Maybe someone says to you, "Why are you so impatient?" And you snap back, "I am not impatient!" Well, you just were! This is why we very seldom believe a criticism of ourselves. Whether the criticism is constructive or not constructive, we always feel small and misunderstood, and sometimes we even fight back.

Many of us never reach higher degrees of prayer because we fight against God's criticism of us in the present moment. This is always a constructive criticism, though. Perhaps the Lord puts us in a state of dryness because He wants us to rise above our selfishness, which forever desires gratification and consolations. As it says in Hebrews, "My son, when the Lord corrects you, do not treat it lightly; but do not get discouraged when he reprimands you. For the Lord trains the ones that he loves and he punishes all those that he acknowledges as his sons" (Heb. 12:5–6). Our poor human nature cannot fathom why God has to permit something challenging in our lives—but faith accepts even when it doesn't understand. Don't worry if you doubt; don't worry if you don't understand. It makes your faith purer if you are confused but still reach out to God, saying, "Lord, I don't understand!" There's nothing that ever said we have to understand—only that we accept the Will of God in the present moment.

When we don't do this, we spend our whole lives struggling to appear to be something we're not. And so we never arrive at self-knowledge. But just as self-knowledge in this world strikes fear into our hearts, self-knowledge in the Kingdom will give us glory, because we will understand all. We will understand that, even though we fought against knowing ourselves and committed sins, we no longer have anything to fear. There will be no fear in Heaven. Some of us live in such fear: We fear our past, we fear our future, and we fear our present. And so, when someone points out our faults, we become very uncomfortable; fear grips our hearts, even to the point of blocking out the beautiful image of God. In Heaven, the masks that we have worn—and we all wear some kind of mask—are going to be discarded. We will be fully, totally free.

Sometimes I imagine what it's going to be like to be totally free, without worrying about human respect, without fear of the future, without wondering what's going to happen tomorrow, without bringing up the past all the time. We get so frustrated in this life: "Why did this happen to me? I was so good! I prayed! I tithed! Why?" In Heaven, we'll know. In Heaven, that doubt and fear will be gone.

We will also no longer have to fear our evil inclinations in Heaven, because they will be gone. So many of us fight to eliminate some inclination that regularly causes us to fall into sin, and sometimes we get tired of fighting. Sometimes we get tired of trying to be good, because no matter how hard we try, just when we think we've conquered it, all of a sudden it comes back. Perhaps, like St. Paul, you struggle with your temper, and weeks may pass, and you think you've mastered it. But then something happens—milk spills or a child whines one too many times—and *boom*, there it is again. Some of us may have even more serious inclinations that we're really scared to death of. Well, in Heaven, we'll know why the Lord permitted us to live with those struggles for so many years. We'll know why we struggled, and we'll understand the merit we received from struggling so hard. And in Heaven, the struggle will be gone. In Heaven, all those good choices you've made for God, rather than for yourself and your pleasure, will earn tremendous glory in the Kingdom that you can't understand now.

St. Paul assures us in Second Corinthians that "it is not ourselves that we are preaching, but Christ Jesus" (2 Cor. 4:5). He continues, "It is the same God that said, 'Let there be light shining out of darkness,' who has shone in our minds to radiate the light of the knowledge of God's glory, the glory on the face of Christ" (2 Cor. 4:6). That's the way it's going to be in Heaven. There's so much assurance in the Kingdom. There are times when we pray for something, but it seems to go from bad to worse. And we just can't understand what's going wrong—why God seems to be ignoring us or, worse, toying with us. But in Heaven, there won't be any more doubts. We will know and understand why it took so long for our prayers to be answered.

On the brighter side, there's never going to be an end to the new things we'll learn in the Kingdom. Right now, the Seraphim, the highest choir of angels, are learning things about God they never knew before. I think one of the most invigorating feelings in the world is the arrival of new knowledge—that light we get from the Lord. Sometimes we get it when we're reading Scripture, when all of a sudden we see something we never saw before, and it's so obvious! In Heaven, we will constantly be learning new things about God. And our lack of knowledge will never be frustrating, as it is on earth. There will be many people in the Kingdom who are smarter than we are, but it won't matter. Here we're envious. But there, everyone's cup will be full. We will rejoice in others' excellence just as they rejoice in ours. And when we learn something, we'll share it with someone else without hesitation or jealousy.

St. Thomas Aquinas said that the different choirs of angels are always sharing their knowledge with each other. You see, in Heaven, it won't matter that there is someone up there higher in rank or more knowledgeable or whatever. It won't even matter if the persons we despised most on earth are higher in the Kingdom than we are! In Heaven, God will be so much to us that all those earthly jealousies won't matter. We'll be content to know whatever God wants us to know—and because we'll always be learning something new, it won't matter that others have much more knowledge.

One of the most beautiful things in Heaven will be that all the mysteries of Scripture will be open to us. Here, sometimes we read a commentary to try to understand a hard verse better, but we just end up more confused! But in Heaven it won't be that way. Not only will all the mysteries of Scripture be made clear, but we'll understand every sense of the Word of God—literal and mystical and symbolic.

And we'll also understand the points in our lives when particular passages or other intercessions changed us. Did you ever have a desire to be better, to be holy, to be like Jesus, but did not know where it came from? In Heaven, you'll know! It may have been a person who prayed for you. It may be your mother; it may be some stranger in

What Is Heaven?

Timbuktu; it may have been a passage you read in Scripture a year ago that suddenly bore fruit.

In Heaven, we'll see how much Jesus loved us — individually, as if no one else existed. We shouldn't waste time wishing God loved us. He does! To prove it, we'll see His wounds in the Kingdom. Some people ask me why I always wear a crucifix. Well, I need to be reminded how much He loves me. Why? Because I have pain and problems and responsibilities — and I can't handle that by myself, and neither can you. So, I have to give love for love. When I think it's all just too much, I look at this, and I say, "It's okay, Lord."

Let's get back to St. Paul, specifically his letter to the Ephesians. He says, "May the God of our Lord Jesus Christ, the Father of glory, give you a spirit of wisdom and perception of what is revealed, to bring you to full knowledge of him. May he enlighten the eyes of your mind so that you can see what hope his call holds for you, what rich glories he has promised the saints will inherit and how infinitely great is the power that he has exercised for us believers. This you can tell from the strength of his power at work in Christ, when he used it to raise him from the dead and to make him sit at his right hand, in heaven, far above every Sovereignty, Authority, Power, or Domination" (Eph. 1:17–21).

We're going to see all that! And in the Kingdom, our very love for one another will be a source of knowledge. We're going to know how God was so loving, and provident, and merciful in each other's lives. There will be virtues and talents in our neighbors that will increase our knowledge of God.

In the first chapter of his letter to the Philippians, St. Paul says, "My prayer is that your love for each other may increase more and more and never stop improving your knowledge and deepening your perception so that you can always recognize what is best" (Phil. 1:9–10). Here St. Paul is talking about arriving at that degree of prayer and holiness *in this life*. And he's talking to everybody! Too often we isolate holiness to special people we call saints. But if you're living a good Christian life, then you are a saint! Saints aren't just ancient figures with polished halos. And anyways, those saints were just as imperfect as you are. They had the same problems and temptations and weaknesses you have. They may have lived in a different century, but every century has its problems. So, we can be saints too, and in Heaven, we will learn from those who came before us, as they will learn from us.

In Heaven, we'll understand the role we played in the salvation of others and in salvation history. Everyone who exists plays a role in salvation history. Whether we like it or not, we influence others every day of our lives. St. Francis would walk through villages in his rough brown garments, turn around, and walk back without saying a word. Our example speaks louder than thousands of words. In Heaven, we will not only know about our influence, but we will meet the people we influenced, the people we, with God's grace, led in the right direction.

So many parents are heartsick over their children who have gotten entangled in drugs, sex, bad crowds, and so on. They pray and pray, and they feel they aren't getting anywhere. And maybe even they die, and it doesn't seem as if anything had changed. But in Heaven, we'll know how powerful our prayers were, how God heard and listened to every prayer. He saw and heard and very slowly led those loves ones in the right direction. And then we will see them face-to-face in the Kingdom, and they will say, "Thank you, Mother. Thank you, Father. I know I gave you a fit. I thank you for your prayers. They saved me. They obtained grace for me. Thank you." So, never, never give up on your children! And children: Never give up on your parents!

Another joy in eternity is that every instant will be fresh. Here we get bored very easily. We can even get tired of smiling! But in Heaven, we'll never again be tired of joy. There will always be some new piece of knowledge, some new experience of God, to rejoice in!

On this earth, we can acquire something of the knowledge and wisdom of God, and we can use it here by sharing it, by inventing things, by improving others' lives. But the knowledge that we have in the Kingdom will be much more glorious because, while our knowledge only skims the surface right now, there we will enter into the very Mind of God.

Chapter 7

∞

Death, the Body, and the Soul

∞

Most of us have a mistaken concept of death. We talk about death as if it's the end of everything, because all the material things we have in life will go. We might understand that death is a calling forth of the soul from the body, but since many of us don't really have any idea what happens to the soul, we focus on what happens to the body: it decays; it returns to dust; little wormies come after it; and all those horrible things. That's what makes death so obnoxious to us.

Well, the first Christians didn't think that way. Even when they saw those big lions come after them in the arena, they were thinking of what would happen to their souls — in Heaven — not to their bodies; otherwise, they would never have had the courage to face those lions. I'm convinced it's because we don't talk enough about Heaven, and because we don't desire Heaven, and because we don't have any idea what happens in Heaven, that we cling to the misery of this world. In reality, death is a passing from one life to another. So, actually, there is no death. Complete death happens to animals and plants; even the mountains fall away. That's death; there's no coming back.

Now, animals do have souls—but the soul of an animal needs the body to continue to exist. When the body dies, the soul dies. Actually, the soul is annihilated. But humans are just the opposite. We are only complete human beings with a soul and a body, but our soul operates the body; it does not need the body. As such, it exists without the body or with the body. The soul requires nothing but God to continue to exist, and so it can exist for centuries, for eons without the body—until, as we will talk about later, the general resurrection.

When we think about the reality of the soul, it's important to remember that Jesus and the early Christians called death "sleep." Remember when Jesus was brought to Jairus's daughter? He said, "She is asleep," and they laughed at Him (see Mark 5:39–40; Luke 8:52–53). And when Lazarus died, Jesus told the disciples, "He is asleep" (see John 11:11). Jesus called it sleep because, in death, the body is in repose. It is still and waiting. It is no longer animated, or made alive, by the soul. When the soul goes, the body becomes cold and incapable of any movement. That's what we've come to call "death."

Now, your soul does have a birthday! It is the day of your conception, and that will be your birthday in the Kingdom. Conception is a real act of God and man, a creation of a body and a soul. It is a time for silent wonder, a time of danger and surprise, a time of love and prayer, a time that begins a wait for the day of accomplishment. In fact, we can compare life to the nine months we spent in our mothers' wombs and can compare death to birth. This is important: Our time in the womb is not a preparation for receiving a soul! We receive our soul at conception! In that sacred act of sacramental union between a man and a woman, God breathes a soul into a new person! The whole process of growth inside the womb, then, is for birth.

Our earthly life is the same way. After birth, the preparation begins again for the next life, the life of eternity. And shortly after birth, if all goes well, there is a kind of new conception, a new birth of life in God: Baptism. When the soul and body have been brought into the world, that soul has to be sanctified by the Holy Spirit. Conception is the necessary start to the process that culminates in birth; Baptism is the necessary start to the process that culminates in Heaven! That's why Catholics baptize children so young. I was born in April but baptized in September, and the priest asked my mother why she didn't just wait until I could walk to church! He was not happy! St. Paul wrote: "If the Spirit of him who raised Jesus from the dead is living in you, then he who raised Jesus from the dead will give life to your own mortal bodies through his Spirit living in you" (Rom. 8:11).

During this journey that we call our lifetime, we must therefore learn to give God our most prized possession: our will. Jesus talked regularly about the Will of God: "I have come to do the Will of the Father" (see John 5:30; 6:38). The first Christians were very conscious of this—so much so that they saw God in everything, even in the lions approaching them, in the persecutions all around them. Let's look at Mark 12, where Our Lord says, "When they rise from the dead, men and women do not marry; no, they are like the angels in heaven" (Mark 12:25). Again, we see that there's a whole new life in Heaven! For His listeners who doubted that they were going to rise again, our Lord continues, "Now about the dead rising again, have you never read in the Book of Moses" ... how God spoke to him and said, 'I am the God of Abraham, the God of Isaac and the God of Jacob'? He is God, not of the dead, but of the living" (Mark 12:26–27). Listen to what Jesus is saying! He is not the God of the dead, but of the living! In Heaven, we live, my friends! We don't die! And our loved ones in Heaven: They live! They have merely transcended this life and gone to the next.

Now, our souls are made up of memory, intellect, and will. These are all going to go on. In Heaven our souls will enjoy what we call the Beatific Vision—seeing God face-to-face. You and I can't even imagine what that means, because no one can see God and live. You can't even look at the sun without going blind: How can you see God and live in this body? So, our souls change as they leave. They are not dead!

In connection with our memory, intellect, and will, there are the virtues of faith, hope, and love. Love is in the will; hope is in the memory; and faith is in the intellect. In Heaven, all of these earthly virtues in our soul will be replaced. Faith will be replaced by vision: We will see God. Hope will be replaced by knowledge: We will no longer have to wonder about Him. And love will go on, though in a more perfect way, because we will possess God. That's why St. Paul said that, of those three virtues, love is the greatest (1 Cor. 13:13).

Now, we've talked about the soul, but the soul is not complete without the body, and the body is nothing but a sack of meat without the soul. We aren't complete people until body and soul are together. At the general resurrection, we'll be made one again.

St. Paul says, "Our homeland is in heaven, and from heaven comes the Savior we are waiting for, the Lord Jesus Christ, and he will transfigure these wretched bodies of ours into copies of his glorious body. He will do that by the same power with which he can subdue the whole universe" (Phil. 3:20–21). Isn't that wonderful? We don't have to worry about all the diseases and disfigurements that were visited upon us in our poor human nature because the real you, the most perfect you, is in the mind of God. And you will rise again. This body, be it ever so corrupted in years to come, will rise again.

In 1 Corinthians 15:52–53, we read, "This will be instantaneous, in the twinkling of an eye, when the last trumpet sounds. It will sound, and the dead will be raised, imperishable, and we shall be changed as well." We might think that we don't want to be changed, but change is part of life! The person you were at six would never recognize you at sixty. But you are the same person. And so, at the general resurrection, that perfect you will be there, "because our present perishable nature must put on imperishability, and our mortal nature, immortality" (see 1 Cor. 15:53).

What exactly will happen to our resurrected bodies? Well, let's look at what happened to the resurrected body of Jesus. The first thing we see about Jesus after the Resurrection is light—and this will also be the first quality of our resurrected bodies. We will be as luminous as the sun! Jesus manifested this quality even before His Resurrection on Mount Tabor at the Transfiguration, and so we will be transfigured, too.

Now, this light will be in degrees. We're not all going to look as bright as everyone else. It all depends on the amount of love we have for God when we die. That was the secret of the first Christians. They knew the resurrected God-Man, and they knew that when they died, no matter how horribly they died, they were going to receive the same glory! And they also knew it was going to depend on how much their will was united to the Will of God, which is just another way of saying how much they loved God. Well, if we recognize that we aren't in the habit of uniting our will to His, then we can always begin right now!

We can see a little bit about this glory of the Lord's Body, and our resurrected body, in Scripture. When St. Stephen was being stoned, he looked up and suddenly he saw this intense brightness: the Son on the right hand of the Father. And Paul was confronted by a tremendous brightness that literally knocked him off his horse. He was blinded by it!

The second quality our bodies will have after resurrection will be incorruption, which means we will never have a disease, an ache, a pain, a headache, indigestion—anything! Our bodies will live forever without decay or deterioration or damage of any kind. It's very difficult for us to understand something truly incorrupt. There are so many things about our body here that are so delicate. But in Heaven, we won't even need to eat—though we will be able to eat. Remember when Our Dear Lord appeared to the Apostles after the Resurrection, and they were petrified? And He said, "Do you have something to eat?" They were flabbergasted that He would think about food at a time like that. But they gave Him fish and a piece of bread. I can imagine those Apostles looking on in awe.

The body will still have its senses, too. The difference is that now our senses rule our will, but in Heaven the will, united with God, will rule the senses. That's part of what it means to be incorrupt. And we'll find that in Jesus.

The third quality that our bodies will have is agility, which means that they will take on the properties of a spirit. Look at John 20:26: "Eight days later the disciples were in the house again and Thomas was with them. The doors were closed, but Jesus came in and stood among them." The Gospel writer keeps telling us the doors were closed, but Jesus appeared in their midst! And we also know that Jesus' tomb was sealed, but He walked through the stone, and then an earthquake came that knocked it over. We'll have that power!

Agility will also enable us to travel with extraordinary swiftness. Our Lord, after the Resurrection, seemed to be everywhere at once: talking to Mary Magdalene, and to the women, and to Peter, and to the disciples going to Emmaus and at the shore. We will be able to travel with our resurrected body at the speed of thought. I could say, "I would like to go to Rome," and, *boom*, there I am! Even better, we'll go anywhere that God wants us to go!

Now, let's look at John again, where Jesus says, "Do not be surprised at this, for the hour is coming when the dead will leave their graves at the sound of his voice: those who did good will rise again to life" (John 5:28–29). It's not only the saved whose bodies will be raised. So you might wonder: "What will the condemned look like?" Put simply, they will be absolutely horrible and grotesque. And that is the choice we have in life between Heaven and Hell. All men will rise at the last day. The demons who fell from the Kingdom will just be spirit, but human beings who have condemned themselves to Hell will rise body and soul in the ugliest bodies you can imagine — and they will be that way forever.

What Is Heaven?

We need to think these sober thoughts when occasions for sin arise. Every time we make a choice for mortal sin, we have made a choice for Hell over Heaven. If we know what we're doing is wrong, and it's serious, and we decide to do it anyway, then we have chosen to be an ugly, grotesque person forever!

You know, I've experienced some pretty difficult things in my life, and even if I were to put them all together in one lump of misery, it would come nowhere near the misery of Hell, where I would be without God for eternity. The Church always asks us to consider the four last things: death, judgment, Heaven, and Hell. We have to think about these things because they're coming, one way or another. There is nothing we can do to stop it! We will live forever and ever! Nothing and no one can terminate your life. The question is: What will that life be like? Earthly death is a transition to one kind of life or another. We may choose Hell, but it's our choice and we will live in it forever. And if we choose Heaven by uniting our wills to God's, we will live there with Him forever.

There, my friends, I hope to see you. We will all have to go through this passing from one life to the next. Let us pray that we will be invited to sing with the angels, "Praise and glory and wisdom and thanksgiving and honor

and power and strength to our God for ever and ever"
(Rev. 7:12).

God bless you! And I love you! May we see each other
in Heaven?

∞

Mother M. Angelica
(1923–2016)

∞

Mother Mary Angelica of the Annunciation was born Rita Antoinette Rizzo on April 20, 1923, in Canton, Ohio. After a difficult childhood, a healing of her recurring stomach ailment led the young Rita on a process of discernment that ended in the Poor Clares of Perpetual Adoration in Cleveland.

Thirteen years later, in 1956, Sister Angelica promised the Lord as she awaited spinal surgery that, if He would permit her to walk again, she would build Him a monastery in the South. In Irondale, Alabama, Mother Angelica's vision took form. Her distinctive approach to teaching the Faith led to parish talks, then pamphlets and books, then radio and television opportunities.

By 1980 the Sisters had converted a garage at the monastery into a rudimentary television studio. EWTN was born. Mother Angelica has been a constant presence on television in the United States and around the world for more than thirty-five years. Innumerable conversions to the Catholic Faith have been attributed to her unique gift for presenting the gospel: joyful but resolute, calming but bracing.

Mother Angelica spent the last years of her life cloistered in the second monastery she founded: Our Lady of the Angels in Hanceville, Alabama, where she and her Nuns dedicated themselves to prayer and adoration of Our Lord in the Most Blessed Sacrament.